AMAZING ANIMALS OF THE WORLD 2

Volume 2

Bunting, Corn — Cricket, Bush

GROLIER

First published 2005 by Grolier, an imprint of Scholastic Library Publishing

For information address the publisher: Grolier, Scholastic Library Publishing
90 Old Sherman Turnpike
Danbury, CT 06816

Set ISBN: 0-7172-6112-3; Volume ISBN: 0-7172-6114-X

Printed and bound in the U.S.A.

Library of Congress Cataloging-in-Publications Data:
Amazing animals of the world 2.
p.cm.
Includes indexes.
Contents: v. 1. Adder—Buffalo, Water -- v. 2. Bunting, Corn—Cricket, Bush -- v. 3. Cricket, European Mole—Frog, Agile -- v. 4. Frog, Burrowing Tree—Guenon, Moustached -- v. 5. Gull, Great Black-backed—Loach, Stone -- v. 6. Locust, Migratory—Newt, Crested -- v. 7. Nuthatch, Eurasian—Razor, Pod -- v. 8. Reedbuck, Mountain—Snake, Tentacled -- v. 9. Snakefly—Toad, Surinam -- v. 10. Tortoise, Gopher—Zebu.
ISBN 0-7172-6112-3 (set : alk. paper) -- ISBN 0-7172-6113-1 (v. 1 : alk. paper) -- ISBN 0-7172-6114-X (v. 2 : alk. paper) -- ISBN 0-7172-6115-8 (v. 3 : alk. paper) -- ISBN 0-7172-6116-6 (v. 4 : alk. paper) -- ISBN 0-7172-6117-4 (v. 5 : alk. paper) -- ISBN 0-7172-6118-2 (v. 6 : alk. paper) -- ISBN 0-7172-6119-0 (v. 7 : alk. paper) -- ISBN 0-7172-6120-4 (v. 8 : alk. paper) -- ISBN 0-7172-6121-2 (v. 9 : alk. paper) -- ISBN 0-7172-6122-0 (v. 10 : alk.paper)
1. Animals--Juvenile literature. I. Title: Amazing animals of the world two. II. Grolier (Firm)
QL49.A455 2005
590--dc22
2005040351

About This Set

Amazing Animals of the World 2 brings you pictures of 400 fascinating creatures and important information about how and where they live.

Each page shows just one species—individual type—of animal. They all fall into seven main categories or groups of animals (classes and phylums scientifically) that appear on each page as an icon or picture—amphibians, arthropods, birds, fish, mammals, other invertebrates, and reptiles. Short explanations of what these group names mean, and other terms used commonly in the set, appear on page 4 in the Glossary.

Scientists use all kinds of groupings to help them sort out the thousands of types of animals that exist today and once wandered here (extinct species). Kingdoms, classes, phylums, genus, and species are among the key words here that are also explained in the Glossary (page 4).

Where animals live is important to know as well. Each of the species in this set lives in a particular place in the world, which you can see outlined on the map on each page. And in those locales the animals tend to favor a particular habitat—an environment the animal finds suitable for life, with food, shelter, and safety from predators that might eat it. There they also find ways to coexist with other animals in the area that might eat somewhat different food, use different homes, and so on. Each of the main habitats is named on the page and given an icon/picture to help you envision it. The habitat names are further defined in the Glossary on page 4.

As well as being part of groups like species, animals fall into other categories that help us understand their lives or behavior. You will find these categories in the Glossary on page 4, where you will learn about carnivores, herbivores, and other types of animals.

And there is more information you might want about an animal—its size, diet, where it lives, and how it carries on its species—the way it creates its young. All these facts and more appear in the data boxes at the top of each page.

Finally, you should know that the set is arranged alphabetically by the most common name of the species. That puts most beetles, say, together in a group so you can compare them easily.

But some animals' names are not so common, and they don't appear near others like them. For instance, the chamois is a kind of goat or antelope. To find animals that are similar—or to locate any species—look in the index at the end of each book in the set (pages 45-48). It lists all animals by their various names (you will find the giant South American river turtle under turtle, giant South American river, and also under its other name—arrau). And you will find all birds, fish, and so on gathered under their broader groupings.

Similarly, smaller like groups appear in the set index as well—butterflies include swallowtails and blues, for example.

Table of Contents
Volume 2

Glossary

Amphibians—species usually born from eggs in water or wet places, which change (metamorphose) into a land animal. Frogs and salamanders are typical. They breathe through their skin mainly and have no scales.

Arctic and Antarctic—icy, cold, dry areas at the ends of the globe that lack trees but see small plants grown in thawed areas (tundra). Penguins and seals are common inhabitants.

Arthropods—animals with segmented bodies, hard outer skin, and jointed legs, such as spiders and crabs.

Birds—born from eggs, these creatures have wings and often can fly. Eagles, pigeons, and penguins are all birds, though penguins can't fly through the air.

Carnivores—they are animals that eat other animals. Many species do eat each other sometimes, and a few eat dead animals. Lions kill their prey and eat it, while vultures clean up dead bodies of animals.

Cities, Towns, and Farms—places where people live and have built or used the land and share it with many species. Sometimes these animals live in human homes or just nearby.

Class—part or division of a phylum.

Deserts—dry, often warm areas where animals often are more active on cooler nights or near water sources. Owls, scorpions, and jack rabbits are common in American deserts.

Endangered—some animals in this set are marked as endangered because it is possible they will become extinct soon.

Extinct—these species have died out altogether for whatever reason.

Family—part of an order.

Fish—water animals (aquatic) that typically are born from eggs and breathe through gills. Trout and eels are fish, though whales and dolphins are not (they are mammals).

Forests and Mountains—places where evergreen (coniferous) and leaf-shedding (deciduous) trees are common, or that rise in elevation to make cool, separate habitats. **Rainforests are different (see below).**

Fresh Water—lakes, rivers, and the like carry fresh water (unlike Oceans and Shores, where the water is salty). Fish and birds abound, as do insects, frogs, and mammals.

Genus—part of a family.

Grasslands—habitats with few trees and light rainfall. Grasslands often lie between forests and deserts, and they are home to birds, coyotes, antelope, and snakes, as well as many other kinds of animals.

Herbivores—these animals eat mainly plants. Typical are hoofed animals (ungulates) that are common on grasslands, such as antelope or deer. Domestic (nonwild) ones are cows and horses.

Hibernators—species that live in harsh areas with very cold winters slow down their functions then and sort of sleep through the hard times.

Kingdom—the largest division of species. Commonly there are understood to be five kingdoms: animals, plants, fungi, protists, and monerans.

Mammals—these creatures usually bear live young and feed them on milk from the mother. A few lay eggs (monotremes like the platypus) or nurse young in a pouch (marsupials like opossums and kangaroos).

Migrators—some species spend different seasons in different places, moving to where more food, warmth, or safety can be found. Birds often do this, sometimes over long distances, but others types of animals also move seasonally, including fish and mammals.

Oceans and Shores—seawater is salty, often deep, and huge. In it live many fish, invertebrates, and even some mammals, such as whales. On the shore birds and other creatures often gather.

Order—part of a class.

Other Invertebrates—animals that lack backbones or internal skeletons. Many, such as insects and shrimp, have hard outer coverings. Clams and worms are also invertebrates.

Phylum—part of a kingdom.

Rainforests—here huge trees grow among many other plants helped by the warm, wet environment. Thousands of species of animals also live in these rich habitats.

Reptiles—these species have scales, lungs to breathe, and lay eggs or give birth to live young. Dinosaurs are thought to have been reptiles, while today the class includes turtles, snakes, lizards, and crocodiles.

Scientific name—the genus and species name of a creature in Latin. For instance, Canis lupus is the wolf. Scientific names avoid the confusion possible with common names in any one language or across languages.

Species—a group of the same type of living thing. Part of an order.

Subspecies—a variant but quite similar part of a species.

Territorial—many animals mark out and defend a patch of ground as their home area. Birds and mammals may call quite small or quite large spots their territories.

Vertebrates—animals with backbones and skeletons under their skins

Corn Bunting
Emberiza calandra

Length: about 7 inches
Diet: mainly seeds, some insects
Home: Europe and northwestern Africa

Number of Eggs: 3 to 4
Order: Perching birds
Family: Buntings and their relatives

 Cities, Towns, and Farms

 Birds

© ROGER TIDMAN / CORBIS

Of the 290 species of bunting in the world, the plump corn bunting is the largest. It is often seen in European gardens and farm fields, hanging from ripe ears of corn. Corn buntings are also common along roadsides and in abandoned fields, where they busily strip the seeds from wild grasses.

As they perch on posts and telephone wires, corn buntings sing a rapid jingle that sounds like someone rattling a ring of keys. In flight, they twitter. Corn buntings are rather awkward and heavy fliers, and often dangle their bright yellow legs as they flutter.

Corn buntings build their nests low to the ground, usually in tall grasses or near the bottom of a thistle bush or hedge. Their

chicks are born completely naked, blind, and helpless. For their first 10 days, the chicks eat insects and grubs, which their parents stuff down their peeping, gaping mouths. By two weeks of age, the young corn buntings have opened their eyes and grown feathers. They then flutter to the ground, where they hunt for seeds with their parents.

No one knows for sure the origin of the name "bunting." It may have come from the German word *bunt*, meaning mottled. This description fits the corn bunting well. Both sexes are speckled in brown, white, and dirty yellow. In the Americas, most of our buntings are known as sparrows and finches. But they are all part of the same family of seed-eating songbirds.

Bushbuck
Tragelaphus scriptus

Length: 3½ to 5 feet
Weight: 55 to 175 pounds
Diet: leaves, buds, fruits, and grasses
Number of Young: 1

Home: sub-Saharan Africa
Order: Even-toed hoofed animals
Family: Bovides

 Forests and Mountains

© S. CHARLES BROWN / FRANK LANE PICTURE AGENCY / CORBIS

Mammals

When most people think of antelope, they imagine gigantic herds of hundreds of animals. But some antelope don't like that much company. The bushbuck is downright antisocial. The typical bushbuck wanders through life alone. It spends most of its time foraging in thick forests. Of course, male and female bushbuck must spend some time together so they can mate. Their courtship involves a special dance. The buck runs up to the doe, his head and neck stretched low. At first, she will cower away. But her suitor follows persistently. He rubs his head against her and licks her, while making a peculiar twittering sound. After mating, the pair rarely stay together. The female gives birth about six months later, and her fawn will

stay by her side for another six months. Then they too will go their separate ways.

The bushbuck's solitary nature once puzzled scientists. Most solitary animals are territorial. That is, they defend the area around their homes from other members of their species. But the home ranges of bushbuck often overlap. When two bushbuck meet, they are generally peaceful.

Out on the savanna, it makes sense for antelope to live in large groups. They can look out for one another and escape from predators by charging across the flat plain. But in a thick forest, a frightened herd of antelope would run crashing into one another. A single bushbuck, however, can quickly dash between the trees.

Brimstone Butterfly
Gonepteryx rhamni

Wingspan: 2 to 2¼ inches
Diet: leaves of buckthorn and other shrubs
Method of Reproduction: egg layer

Home: Europe, Asia, and North Africa
Order: Butterflies and moths
Family: Whites, sulphurs, and orange tips

 Cities, Towns, and Farms

 Arthropods

© FRANCESC MUNTADA / CORBIS

The brimstone butterfly is named for the bright yellow wings of the male. The female is very easy to distinguish from the male—her wings are a pale greenish-white. However, both the male and the female have a small orange spot on each wing.

The brimstone butterfly prefers to live in open places such as gardens and fields. When it flies about, its brightly colored wings are spread wide. But as soon as it settles on a plant or on the ground, it folds its wings to cover its back. By doing this the brimstone butterfly can fool a predator, like a bird, who may think that the butterfly is just a leaf rather than a tasty insect. The butterfly can live in mountain altitudes up to 6,000 feet. In northern Europe and other places with chilly winters, the butterfly hibernates until warm weather arrives.

After mating in the spring, the female lays her eggs on the buds or the undersides of young leaves. The caterpillars that hatch from these eggs are green and covered with short hairs. The green coat provides excellent camouflage for the caterpillars, who blend in easily with the leaves upon which they feed. The caterpillars eat and grow for several weeks and then use a silk thread to attach themselves to plants. They enter the pupal stage, during which they metamorphose, or change, into adult brimstone butterflies.

Sail Butterfly (Scarce Swallowtail)
Iphiclides podalirius

Length: up to 1½ inches
Diet: leaves (caterpillar); flower nectar (adult)
Method of Reproduction: egg layer

Wingspan: 2⅓ to 3⅓ inches
Home: Europe, Asia, and northern Africa
Order: Butterflies and moths
Family: Swallowtails

Forests and Mountains

Arthropods

© NATURFOTO HONAL / CORBIS

From April to July, the beautiful sail butterfly flits over bright flower meadows. Less frequently it makes its home in hilly farm communities or on the sunny southern slopes of low mountains. The butterfly is named for the sail-like shape of its extremely broad front wings.

The sail butterfly's other name—the scarce swallowtail—refers to its rarity compared to other members of its family. The species is threatened with extinction because people have cut down many of the hawthorn and blackthorn shrubs that the butterfly caterpillars eat. To prevent the extinction of this much-loved insect, several European countries have established protected areas where it can live undisturbed.

After mating, females lay eggs, singly, on the leaves of blackthorn, hawthorn, plum, pear, and apple trees. When the eggs hatch in mid- to late summer, the caterpillars begin feeding on the leaves. Each caterpillar has a characteristic forked bump behind its head that looks like a set of tiny antlers. These horns are brightly colored and have a distinctive odor.

In fall the caterpillar spins a chrysalis, or cocoon. Inside this hard case, it sleeps through the winter. By spring the caterpillar has transformed into an adult butterfly that breaks out of its cocoon.

Freshwater Butterflyfish
Pantodon buchholzi

Length: up to 4 inches
Diet: insects
Method of Reproduction: egg layer
Home: west-central Africa

Order: Bony-tongues, mooneyes, and their relatives
Family: Freshwater butterflyfishes

 Fresh Water

 Fish

On a sweltering day in tropical Africa, small, stagnant ponds seem ready to boil with the heat. The only things moving over the dank green water are giant, buzzing mosquitoes. Suddenly a fist-sized ball of fins and spines leaps from the water, thrashing in the air. The mosquitoes scatter, but it's too late. The freshwater butterflyfish swallows several of them before it splashes back into the murky water.

When the freshwater butterflyfish leaps from the water, it flaps its large, winglike pectoral fins. In this way, it can propel itself through the air for nearly 5 feet! The butterflyfish feeds by gulping down insects that have fallen onto the water's surface. Its large mouth opens toward the top of its head, allowing the butterflyfish to easily slurp down prey from below.

The weedy ponds, ditches, and lakes that the butterflyfish calls home are as warm as bathwater. Such dank water contains little oxygen. The butterflyfish survives by coming to the surface for air and using its swim-bladder as a simple lung. Many fish gulp air into their swim-bladder to help them float. But only a few species, such as the butterflyfish, can also breathe in this way.

The fantastic-looking freshwater butterflyfish is a popular but expensive aquarium pet. It comes in a convenient size, and its weird appearance and lively behavior are sure to entertain.

Ceylonese Caecilian
Ichthyophis glutinosus

Length: 12 to 16 inches
Diet: earthworms, insects, and spiders
Number of Eggs: up to 24

Home: Sri Lanka
Order: Caecilians
Family: Ichthyophiid caecilians

 Rainforests

 Amphibians

© TOM MCHUGH / PHOTO RESEARCHERS

When most people think of amphibians, images of frogs or salamanders usually come to mind. However, there is a third, less familiar order of amphibians called the *Caecilians*. A typical representative of this order is a legless, burrowing creature that looks like a large earthworm. Its head is hard and bony, and its long, round body is divided into hundreds of ringed segments. Although common in tropical regions, caecilians are seldom seen, because they surface only at night or in the rain.

The Ceylonese caecilian is found in only one small part of the world—on the island of Sri Lanka, which was once called Ceylon. It resembles a small snake, with a bright yellow stripe on both sides of its body. Like all caecilians, this species has very tiny eyes covered by a thin layer of skin. It has a crude sense of sight, unlike most caecilians, which are totally blind.

Ceylonese caecilians burrow in muddy ground close to swamps, ponds, and streams. The male fertilizes the female's eggs through an opening in her body. She then tunnels close to a pond or stream, where she lays a clutch of eggs. The mother does not leave them until they hatch. The newborn immediately head for the water. Like tadpoles, immature caecilians swim about and breathe through gills. Only after they metamorphose into air-breathing adults do the young crawl out of the water and burrow into the earth.

Common Carp
Cyprinus carpio

Length: 1 to 2½ feet
Weight: 10 to 60 pounds
Diet: flora and small invertebrates
Method of Reproduction: egg layer

Home: native to Japan, China, and Central Asia—introduced throughout the world
Order: Minnows, suckers, and shadlike fishes
Family: Carps and minnows

 Fresh Water

 Fish

© Y. LANCEAU / JACANA / PHOTO RESEARCHERS

There are 10 subspecies of carp, originally all from East Asia, Siberia, and Europe. The fish has now been introduced throughout the world and is bred commercially. Total world catch exceeds 200,000 tons per year. Wild carp are found most often in large rivers. The Romans introduced the carp into much of northern and western Europe.

The carp is olive to yellow-green with rust-colored sides. Its color is brighter in rivers and darker in mud ponds. It has no teeth in its mouth, but has three sets of throat teeth. These throat teeth grind food against a hard pad on the lower part of the skull.

The carp becomes sexually mature within three or four years. A very fertile fish, the female can produce over 60,000 eggs per pound of body weight. Some large females produce up to 1.5 million eggs. Egg laying, beginning in May or June, takes place on soft plants or in warm, shallow waters. A female may spawn several times during the summer. The eggs develop in three to five days. In winter, carp stop feeding and enter a rest period similar to hibernation.

Carp were introduced into the United States in 1880, but they proved harmful to our native fish populations. In one Wisconsin lake, carp completely eliminated the resident fish population. They are a popular game and food fish in Europe.

European Wild Cat
Felis silvestris

Length: 32 to 48 inches (including tail)
Height at the Shoulder: 10 to 14 inches
Weight: 7 to 18 pounds
Diet: mainly small rodents

Number of Young: 2 to 4
Home: Europe and western Asia
Order: Carnivores
Family: Cats

 Forests and Mountains

 Mammals

© HANS REINHARD / BRUCE COLEMAN INC.

The European wild cat is about the same size as a large domestic cat.

Outwardly, the European wild cat has a bigger head and larger teeth than its domestic cousin. In its everyday habits, the European wild cat is definitely wild and a fierce hunter. In the cool forests of Europe and Asia, this creature runs quickly and climbs well. The wild cat spends much time in the treetops, moving quietly from one branch to another in its hunt for birds and squirrels.

European wild cats usually live alone. Even the females chase off their young once the kittens are able to care for themselves. Each wild cat has its own territory, which may cover an area of 1 square mile or more. To mark its territory, the European wild cat uses two kinds of markers. Between the pads of its feet are scent glands. As the wild cat travels through the forest, it leaves behind a trail of scent. The wild cat also leaves claw scratches on tree trunks. Other cats smell the scent and see the scratches. These signs warn them that the owner of the territory is nearby.

European wild cats mate in spring. The female gives birth in a den about three months after mating. The kittens weigh 3 to 5 ounces at birth and feed on their mother's milk for several months. During this time the mother teaches them how to hunt and defend themselves. As soon as the kittens are old enough, the mother leaves them, and the young ones are left on their own to survive in the wild.

Geoffroy's Cat
Leopardus geoffroyi

Length of the Body: 18 to 30 inches

Length of the Tail: 10 to 14 inches

Weight: up to 18 pounds

Diet: small mammals and birds

Number of Young: 1 to 3

Home: South America

Order: Carnivores

Family: Cats

 Grasslands

 Mammals

© ROD WILLIAMS / BRUCE COLEMAN INC.

Geoffroy's is a small, slender cat with a thick, spotted coat. It lives in the bushy foothills and grasslands at the base of the Andes Mountains in Peru and Argentina. The South Americans call this cat *gato montes*, meaning "bush cat."

The daily habits of Geoffroy's cat are largely unknown. Like other small, wild cats, it probably hunts at night. Its prey includes a variety of small mammals and birds. It has no natural enemies, but in recent years it has attracted the attention of fur trappers. In the past, hunters preferred to kill ocelots and other spotted cats with more valuable fur. When ocelots became rare, the hunters began killing Geoffroy's cats. This species is now protected by many South American governments. Nonetheless, poachers continue to kill many of these cats illegally.

There are several subspecies, or races, of Geoffroy's cat. They vary in appearance from the northern part of the cat's range to the south. In northern Argentina, Geoffroy's cats weigh less than 10 pounds and have reddish-yellow fur. These northern cats have many small spots that blend together to form stripes. In the cooler climate of South America's southern tip, Geoffroy's cats may weigh as much as 18 pounds. To survive snowy winters, they have especially long, soft fur that is grayish-silver with large, round spots. All Geoffroy's cats have a beautiful ringed tail.

Iriomote Cat
Prionailurus iriomotensis

Length of the Body: about 2 feet

Length of the Tail: about 8 inches

Height at the Shoulder: about 1 foot

Weight: about 12 pounds

Diet: small animals

Number of Young: unknown

Home: Iriomote Island, Japan

Order: Carnivores

Family: Cats

 Forests and Mountains

 Mammals

 Endangered Animals

© TADAAKI IMAIZUM / PHOTO RESEARCHERS

Scientists discovered the Iriomote cat on a small Japanese island in 1966. By then it was already quite rare. About the size of a large house cat, the Iriomote has dark grayish-brown fur with black spots and circles. Biologists believe that this species is the oldest of all living cats. Unfortunately, it is estimated that fewer than 40 Iriomote cats are still alive.

The last surviving Iriomote cats are found only on one small Japanese island, from which they take their name. Barely 108 miles square, Iriomote Island is the westernmost of a chain of islands called the Ryukyus. The cat shares its small home with numerous farmers, who grow rice and other crops in the lowland valleys. Human encroachment is likely responsible for the increasing rarity of this cat.

At present, the species seems destined for extinction. Although Japan has established a national park on Iriomote Island, the protected areas include only mountainous regions. The Iriomote cat must hunt along lowland streams and rivers to find its prey. Its diet consists largely of small rodents, birds, and probably fish, frogs, and crabs.

Little else is known about this animal. Like most wild cats, it leads a solitary life. Its footprints are most often seen on the edges of swamps and streams. Experts believe the cat spends most of its time on the ground, although it does climb into trees.

Ring-tailed Cat
Bassariscus astutus

Length of the Body: 12 to 15 inches

Length of the Tail: 12½ to 17½ inches

Diet: insects, eggs, small rodents, fruits, and nectar

Weight: about 2¼ pounds

Number of Young: 1 to 4

Home: western North America

Order: Carnivores

Family: Raccoons

  Forests and Mountains

Mammals

© KEVIN SCHAFER / CORBIS

As its name might suggest, the ring-tailed cat moves like a cat, sits like a cat, and washes itself like a cat. But one look at its long, bushy black-and-white ringed tail tells you that this creature's name is misleading. The ring-tailed cat is a member of the raccoon family. Ring-tailed cats are easy to tame. Early settlers of the American West even kept them as pets. People living in mining camps used ring-tailed cats as mouse catchers.

Ring-tailed cats live in forests, meadows, and dry, rocky places, from sea level to elevations of 9,500 feet. They are shy, solitary animals that rest during the day under rocks or in dens in hollow trees. Ringtails have excellent eyesight and

hearing, senses they put to good use when they head out at night to hunt. They usually find their favorite foods on the ground, but will climb trees if a tasty morsel, such as an insect or rodent, is beyond their grasp. When threatened, ringtails hiss, snarl, and even bark. They also produce a foul-smelling secretion that is sure to repel even the hardiest of enemies. If all else fails, ring-tailed cats raise the hairs on their tail, making the tail look bigger than the body.

Ringtails mate in early spring. The babies weigh about 9 ounces at birth and feed on their mother's milk until they are four months old. The young grow fast; they are almost full-grown at the age of five months. Ring-tailed cats can live up to 16 years.

Bronze Catfish
Corydoras aeneus

Length: up to 2¾ inches
Diet: water fleas and other small invertebrates
Method of Reproduction: egg layer

Home: streams in northern South America
Order: Catfishes
Family: Mailed catfishes

  Fresh Water

Fish

© JANE BURTON / BRUCE COLEMAN INC.

When you think of a fish's home, you usually think of water. The bronze catfish does live in streams. But when the stream begins to dry up, the catfish pulls itself out of the water. Then it moves across land in search of another stream. The fish breathes on land by swallowing air into its digestive system, where oxygen is passed into the bloodstream.

Each side of the bronze catfish's body is jacketed with two rows of bony plates, called mail, which overlap like tiles on a roof. This suit of armor gives the head and back of this small brown fish a sparkling metallic look. Both sexes look alike, although the female is larger than the male.

Bronze catfish live in small groups called shoals. They rest in one spot on the bottom of a slow-flowing stream, using their fins to anchor themselves in place. At feeding time the catfish rely on two small feelers, or barbels, on either side of their mouth to find fleas and other food in the dark.

Barbels also play a role during mating season. The male catfish holds on to a female's barbels with his fins until she lays several eggs that she keeps on her ventral, or abdominal, fin. The male then releases his sperm and lets go of the female. She swims through the cloud of sperm, which fertilizes the eggs, and deposits the sticky eggs on objects on the bottom of the stream. The eggs hatch about one week later.

Congo Catfish
Synodontis nigriventris

Length: 2 to 4 inches
Diet: algae and insects
Method of Reproduction: egg layer

Home: Central Africa
Order: Catfish
Family: Mochokids

 Fresh Water

 Fish

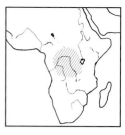

© YVETTE TAVERNIEW / BIOS / PETER ARNOLD, INC.

The first time you see this fish, you'll probably find it strange. The whiskers around its mouth and its sharp spikes make it look like the common catfish. But, unlike other fish, the Congo catfish has a light back and a dark belly. This strange coloration makes sense when you know that the Congo catfish is used to swimming on its back! That way it can feed on leaves and dead wood floating on the water's surface.

Fishes' backs are usually darker than their bellies because the sunlight comes from above. If you look at the fish sideways underwater, its dark back and light belly seem to be the same color since the back looks lighter from the sunshine and the belly is in the shade. When you look up at it from below, it is hard to see its light belly against the surface light. When Congo catfish began to feed by swimming upside down, their coloration changed too.

Catfish live in the Congo River, in Africa. They scrape algae from the bottom of plants or dead branches. They also eat insect larvae or small aquatic insects, which they find with their whiskers. They are not afraid of predators because the sharp spines on their fins protect them. The Congo catfish is a popular tropical fish that is easy to keep in a heated aquarium. It needs dim light; and if there are plants floating on the surface, the fish tends to swim on its back. This is fun to watch!

Glass Catfish
Kryptopterus bichirrhus

Length: up to 4 inches
Diet: plankton
Method of Reproduction: egg layer

Home: Southeast Asia
Order: Catfishes
Family: Eurasian catfishes

 Fresh Water

 Fish

© JANE BURTON / BRUCE COLEMAN INC.

The glass catfish is a living anatomy lesson—you don't have to dissect it to see every bone and organ in its body. Its fascinating see-through body and its peaceable nature make this fish a popular pet for tropical freshwater aquariums. But, unlike most catfish, this species is not a scavenger.

For some reason, glass catfish do not breed in captivity. Perhaps aquarium life does not provide the right physical conditions for their eggs. Or perhaps glass catfish need certain visual cues—seen only in nature—to put them in the mood for mating. As a result, all the glass catfish sold in pet stores have to be flown from Southeast Asia, where they are harvested from rainforest streams.

In the wild, glass catfish occupy a very specific place, or niche, in their environment. They swim halfway between the surface and the bottom of a stream. There they hunt small invertebrates, called plankton, which can barely be seen without a microscope. The catfish, in turn, are preyed upon by many large fish.

To sense the approach of enemies, glass catfish rely on a special sense organ called a Weberian apparatus. It is a small chain of bones near the fish's spine. Through it the catfish can sense movement and sound in the water. In this way the catfish is warned of approaching predators even before it can see them.

Shovelnose Catfish
Sorubium lima

Length: 2 feet
Diet: small fish and crustaceans
Method of Reproduction: egg layer

Home: streams in eastern South America
Order: Catfishes
Family: South American pimelodid catfishes

 Fresh Water

 Fish

© MARK SMITH / PHOTO RESEARCHERS

Like all catfish, the shovelnose variety has three pairs of long feelers, or barbels, which look like the whiskers of a cat. But perhaps more remarkable is the creature's broad, duckbill-like snout, a feature from which the shovelnose gained its name. On the underside of the snout is the shovelnose's mouth. The mouth's location serves the creature well at feeding time. Like a vacuum cleaner, the shovelnose uses its mouth to suck up crustaceans and other goodies as it moves along the river bottom.

During the day the shovelnose catfish lies hidden among leaves and other debris on the river bottom. But as evening falls, it begins its hunt for food, an activity that continues throughout the night. This creature depends on its sense of touch and on its taste buds to find food. In fact, the barbels are covered with taste buds—just like a human tongue! As the catfish moves along the river bottom, its barbels constantly move back and forth, picking up information about the environment.

The shovelnose catfish is silver-gray, with a white belly. Unlike most fish, the shovelnose's skin is bare, completely lacking scales. Its dorsal fins (on the top of the body) and pectoral fins (on the sides behind the gills) have no color and are covered with strong spines. The sharp spines are weapons of defense, providing protection against other fish that might find the shovelnose catfish a tasty dinner.

Blind Cavefish
Astyanax mexicanus jordani

Length: up to 3½ inches
Method of Reproduction: egg layer
Home: North America and Central America

Diet: plant and animal matter
Order: Carps and their relatives
Family: Characins

  Fresh Water

Fish

© MARK SMITH / PHOTO RESEARCHERS

The blind cavefish lives in subterranean (underground) streams and pools. This odd-looking creature has only the remnants of eyes, buried beneath the shiny pink skin of its face. Through these half-formed peepers, the cavefish can sense only light, which it avoids.

Most blind cavefish can be found near the Mexican city of San Luis Potosí. They were once considered a unique species. But biologists now agree that the blind cavefish is just one subspecies of a larger species called the Mexican tetra. Most Mexican tetras have normal eyes and live in aboveground waters from Texas and New Mexico through central Mexico.

Although they cannot see, blind cavefish have a good sense of where they are. They navigate through the darkness using their keen senses of touch and smell. They usually swim restlessly, head down, snuffling through the stream bottom for food. They are scavengers and eat just about anything, alive or dead.

When they are ready to breed, the male and female circle one another for several hours. The male pulls alongside his mate and vibrates his body as he presses against her. The pair then swim to the surface of the water, where they spawn. The fertilized eggs hatch three or four days later. At birth, the young have small, functional eyes; they lose their sight as they mature.

Chamois
Rupicapra rupicapra

Length of the Body: 3½ to 4½ feet
Length of the Tail: 4 to 6 inches
Diet: grass, leaves, and other plant matter

Weight: 30 to 135 pounds
Number of Young: usually 1
Home: mountains of Europe
Order: Even-toed hoofed mammals
Family: Bovines

 Forests and Mountains

 Mammals

© MANFRED DANEGGER / PETER ARNOLD, INC.

Endangered Animals

The chamois (pronounced 'sham-ē) is a small, goatlike antelope with short, sharply hooked horns. This creature is exceptionally sure-footed—an important adaptation to its high mountain home, where putting a foot in the wrong place could mean slipping and falling to a sure death. Fortunately, the chamois can jump easily from one rocky ledge to another. People have seen chamois standing, with all four feet close together, on rocky points no bigger around than a coffee cup.

Female chamois and their young live in herds. Adult males live alone except during the mating season. At that time the males often butt and chase one another, occasionally using their horns as weapons. The baby chamois, called a kid, weighs between 7 and 11 pounds at birth. It can walk shortly after it is born—even before its fur has dried.

In summer, chamois have a light-colored coat about 1½ inches long. The winter coat is up to 8 inches long and blackish brown. Chamois have excellent eyesight. It is their most important sense because they must keep a sharp eye out for lynx, wolves, bears, and other enemies. If a chamois senses danger, it alerts other members of the herd by whistling through its nose or by stamping its feet.

The chamois was the original source for chamois leather, a soft material used to dry and polish furniture, automobiles, and other items. Today chamois leather is made from the skins of domestic sheep and goats.

Water Chevrotain
Hyemoschus aquaticus

Length: up to 40 inches
Weight: 22 to 33 pounds
Diet: mainly fruit
Number of Young: 1
Home: West Africa

Order: Even-toed hoofed mammals
Family: Mouse deer and water
Suborder: Ruminants

 Forests and Mountains

 Mammals

The water chevrotain is a small, graceful animal that looks somewhat like a deer, though it does not have horns or antlers. It has a small head with a pointed snout, a short tail, and long, slender legs. Its brown coat is decorated with white spots and lines. Males have two enlarged teeth, or tusks, in their upper jaw.

Water chevrotains are shy, nocturnal animals that inhabit dense forests, staying near bodies of water. During the day, they rest under large leaves or among dense tropical plants. At night, they come out to feed on fruit and other plant matter. If there is danger, they jump into the water and disappear. They swim underwater until they reach bushes and overhanging vines that will hide them from their predators. Their main enemies are people who hunt chevrotains for food. Hunting has greatly reduced the number of these defenseless creatures.

Except during the mating season, water chevrotains live alone. When two chevrotains meet, they communicate by means of sounds and smell. A female gives birth to one offspring at a time, after a gestation period of six to nine months. She does not spend much time with her baby, who is usually left alone until feeding time. The mother nurses her baby for three to six months.

Black-capped Chickadee
Parus atricapillus

Length: 4¾ to 5¾ inches
Wingspan: 7½ to 8½ inches
Weight: about ⅓ ounce
Diet: insects, spiders, millipedes, snails, seeds, and fruits

Number of Eggs: 5 to 10
Home: United States and Canada
Order: Perching birds
Family: Titmice and chickadees

Forests and Mountains

Birds

© WAYNE LANKINEN / BRUCE COLEMAN INC.

Unlike most birds, which shy away from people, the black-capped chickadee loves to be around humans, their gardens, and their birdhouses. It may even eat out of your hands—especially if those hands contain walnuts or other tasty tidbits. At bird feeders, it prefers sunflower seeds and peanut butter. If you want to attract lots of chickadees to your bird feeder during the winter, keep it stocked with seeds and suet, since food is scarce in the wild at that time of year.

This chickadee is named for the black cap of feathers on its head. Males and females look alike. The name "chickadee" comes from the bird's call, "chick-a-dee-dee-dee." The bird also whistles "fee-bee."

If a person hears a chickadee and imitates its notes, the bird will likely answer.

A pair of black-capped chickadees makes its nest in a tree hole, in a rotted branch or stump, or even an abandoned woodpecker hole. The female lines the nest with plant fibers, wool, and other soft materials. Both parents take turns incubating the eggs, which hatch in about 12 days. If a chickadee is disturbed while it is sitting on the eggs, it hisses like a snake to scare away the intruder.

Baby black-capped chickadees are ready to leave the nest when they are about two weeks old. Some "black caps" migrate southward for the winter, often traveling in flocks that contain thousands of birds.

Greater Prairie Chicken
Tympanuchus cupido

Length: 16½ to 18 inches
Diet: leaves, fruits, grains, and insects
Number of Eggs: 10 to 12
Size of the Egg: 1¾ inches

Home: central North America
Order: Game birds
Family: Pheasants and quails
Subfamily: Grouses

 Grasslands

 Birds

© W. PERRY CONWAY / CORBIS

Greater prairie chickens are famous for their large, loud courtship displays. Each spring the adult males, called roosters, return to a special courtship site, called a "lek." There they dance in large groups from April through May. It is quite a spectacle, with much jumping and stomping.

But the most amazing part of the courtship display is the noise. As he dances, each rooster inflates the bright orange sacs on the sides of his head. When he deflates the sacs, they make a booming noise.

As you might have guessed, all the dancing and noise are designed to attract females, called hens, who walk around the lek and choose their favorite rooster. After mating with a suitor, the female quietly leaves to build her nest. She scrapes a crude hole in the ground—hidden among tall grasses or shrubs—and lines it with dead leaves, feathers, and grass. Only the hen warms the eggs and cares for the chicks.

Sadly, greater prairie chickens are growing rare. One variety, the heath hen of New England, is already extinct. Another variety, Attwater's prairie chicken, which lives in southern Louisiana and Texas, is in danger of extinction. The problem has been the loss of the bird's habitat: North America's tall-grass prairie. This unique ecosystem has largely been destroyed to make way for farms, oil and gas wells, and cities.

Chub
Leuciscus cephalus

Length: up to 31 inches
Diet: insects, smaller fish, frogs, crustaceans, and fish eggs
Method of Reproduction: egg layer

Weight: up to 17 pounds
Home: Europe and Turkey
Order: Carps and their relatives
Family: Carps

 Fresh Water

 Fish

© HANS REINHARD / BRUCE COLEMAN INC.

The chub, with its long, powerful body, is known throughout Europe as a good angling fish. Great skill is needed to catch this large, fighting carp. Unfortunately, its flesh is tasteless and filled with a great many bones. When cooked, chub meat is said to resemble "cotton wool well stuffed with needles." Because it is virtually inedible, the chub is considered a pest in rivers where it competes for food with tasty trout and salmon. Large chub also prey upon these game fish. To their credit, young chub are important food for herons, kingfishers, river otters, and larger trout and pike.

The chub is easily recognized by its large head, big mouth, and thick lips. Because its scales are darkly edged, the fish has a checkered, or crosshatched, appearance. Many chub are metallic bronze or shiny gold. Sometimes there is a reddish-bronze cast on the sides of the head. This European chub should not be confused with its many North American cousins, which are also referred to as chub.

Between April and June, male chub develop small white warts all over their body. This signals their readiness to spawn. Young chub gather in breeding schools near plants and over gravelly, shallow water. The older adults prefer to spawn in pairs. As they spawn, the females deposit their tiny, sticky eggs on stones and vegetation. The eggs hatch in eight to 10 days.

Chuckwalla
Sauromalus obesus

Length: up to 16 inches
Diet: flowers, buds, and other plant matter
Home: southwestern United States

Number of Eggs: about 8
Order: Lizards and snakes
Family: Iguanas
Suborder: Lizards

 Deserts

 Reptiles

© C. K. LORENZ / PHOTO RESEARCHERS

The chuckwalla is a broad, bulky lizard whose thick tail is as long as its head and body. Its dull brown skin is dry and covered with many small scales, giving it the feel of sandpaper. Folds of loose skin are at the sides of the neck and body.

The chuckwalla lives in warm, rocky deserts of the southwestern United States. Its color blends into its surroundings, helping make the chuckwalla "invisible" to enemies. Like all lizards, its body temperature changes with the outside temperature. It spends a lot of time sunning itself on rocks, though it frequently crawls in and out of shady spots to keep from getting too hot. When a chuckwalla is in danger, it crawls into a narrow crevice among the rocks. It gulps lots of air into its lungs, blowing itself up like a balloon. This makes it almost impossible for any enemy to remove the chuckwalla from the crevice.

Chuckwallas are harmless lizards, but they have many enemies, including various birds and snakes. American Indians used to hunt and eat chuckwallas.

Chuckwallas eat flowers and other plant matter. They usually get all the water they need from their food. They mate in early summer, after which the female lays about eight eggs in a hole she digs in the sand.

Firemouth Cichlid
Cichlasoma meeki

Length: up to 6 inches
Diet: small fish and invertebrates
Number of Eggs: 100 to 500

Home: Central America
Order: Perchlike fishes
Family: Cichlids

 Fresh Water

 Fish

© MARK SMITH / PHOTO RESEARCHERS

The brightly colored firemouth cichlid gets its name from its brick-red lower jaw. The male firemouth is especially brilliant, and his back and tail fins are larger and more vibrant than his mate's. In both sexes, all the body scales are trimmed with a red edge.

Not surprisingly, this beautiful freshwater species is a popular aquarium fish. Fortunately, firemouth cichlids breed well in captivity. Their wild population has not been depleted for the pet trade. They get along with most other aquarium fish, except when breeding. At that time, they may eat smaller fish that share their habitat.

In nature, firemouth cichlids are found in warm tropical rivers, ponds, and streams. They also swim underground in subterranean streams that connect natural springs. They cannot survive when water temperatures drop below 68 degrees Fahrenheit.

Like most cichlids, firemouths are attentive parents. Before mating, the couple carefully cleans a rock, where the female then lays her eggs. When they hatch, the baby fish, called fry, cluster together. The parents herd their young into small pits in the streambed or pond bottom. The adults fearlessly chase away intruders. At the same time, they must chase back any fry that wander from the pit. Gradually the growing young firemouths become bolder in their attempts to escape. About the same time, their parents lose interest in guarding them.

Lionhead Cichlid
Steatocranus casuarius

Length: 3¾ inches (male); 2¾ inches (female)
Diet: plant and animal matter
Method of Reproduction: egg layer

Home: Congo River Basin in Africa
Order: Perchlike fishes
Family: Cichlids

 Fresh Water

 Fish

© HANS REINHARD / BRUCE COLEMAN INC.

The male lionhead cichlid has a large cushion of fatty tissue on the top of his head. This "bump" gives the fish an almost serious and stern look, and is the basis of the fish's genus name, *Steatocranus*, which comes from two Greek words meaning "fat skull." This same bump also gave rise to the creature's less complimentary name: the African blockhead!

The lionhead cichlid lives in the rapids of fast-moving streams. Although most fish are good swimmers, the lionhead is an exception. It gets from one place to the next by short jumping movements along the bottom of the stream. There the fish feeds on plant and animal matter.

Lionhead cichlids are shy, peaceful animals until the breeding season arrives. Then the males may become very aggressive toward one another. The female lays her eggs in sheltered spots on the river bottom. She may lay as many as 100 large orange eggs. Her mate fiercely defends the area around the nest. Both parents watch over the eggs and care for the young.

These fish are popular in home aquariums. They require warm water (76 to 80 degrees Fahrenheit) and thrive if a circulation pump helps mix the water with air so that the lionhead's environment is rich in oxygen. The aquarium should have plenty of rocky hiding places that offer sheltered spots for the fish.

Masked Palm Civet
Paguma larvata

Length of the Body: up to 28 inches
Length of the Tail: up to 24 inches
Weight: up to 11 pounds
Diet: fruits and small animals

Number of Young: 2 to 4
Home: southern Asia
Order: Carnivores
Family: Viverrids, aardwolves, and hyenas

 Rainforests

 Mammals

© PETE OXFORD / NATURE PICTURE LIBRARY

The masked palm civet is named for its black-and-white facial markings. Scientists believe that the bold mask may serve as a warning to predators. When attacked, the civet douses its enemy with a foul-smelling spray. Like a skunk, the civet produces the stinky fluid in its anal glands. The spray blinds the attacker momentarily and usually scares it away.

The body of the masked civet is a handsome brown that varies from light to dark. Its tail is darker than its body and ends in a white tip. Like other palm civets, this species has a pointed face like that of a fox.

Masked palm civets are quick and agile climbers. During the night, they travel through the trees, searching for fruits and small prey. They are especially fond of bananas, mangoes, and figs—food for which their dull, wide teeth are well suited. However, the civet occasionally eats meat. In the jungle, it hunts insects, lizards, and small birds. Near villages and towns, the civet has been accused of stealing chickens. But for the most part, it is more interested in garbage than in farm animals.

Little is known about how civets reproduce. This species seems to have two breeding seasons, one in spring and the other in fall. While raising their young, the civets remain together. At all other times, they live alone.

Ring-tailed Coati
Nasua nasua

Length: 30 to 50 inches
Length of Tail: 14 to 26 inches
Weight: 6 to 13 pounds
Diet: insects, lizards, and small rodents

Number of Young: 3 to 7
Home: South America
Order: Carnivores
Family: Raccoons and coatis

 Rainforests

 Mammals

The ring-tailed coati is one of four species of coatimundis that live in the forests of South America. It is closely related to the raccoon, but can be distinguished by its pointed, trunklike snout.

The coati prefers to eat worms and insects, although it also preys on lizards and small rodents. The coati kills its prey by rolling it under the soles of its front feet. In this way, the coati not only kills its prey, but also removes spines and stingers that many insects and lizards use to defend themselves. Sometimes the coati will prepare its insect meal by simply biting off its head!

Coatis are most active during the day. Females and young coatis live in groups of up to 25 animals; adult males live alone. These solitary males join other coatis only during the mating season, which lasts for one month in the winter. During this time, the strongest males keep the weaker ones away from the desirable females.

About 75 days after mating, mothers give birth to their young. The babies are born with their ears and eyes closed, and measure about 10 inches long. After a few weeks, the babies begin to scour the jungle for food with their mother. The female keeps the family together by making a peeping sound that the babies instinctively know to follow. Coatis reach adult size 15 months after birth and live as long as 14 years.

King Cobra
Ophiophagus hannah

Length: up to 18 feet
Weight: 20 pounds
Diet: other snakes
Number of Young: 18 to 40

Home: southern Asia
Order: Lizards and snakes
Family: Terrestrial poisonous
    snakes

 Rainforests

Reptiles

© JOE MCDONALD / VISUALS UNLIMITED

The king cobra is the world's largest poisonous snake. It can grow up to 18 feet in length and weigh as much as 20 pounds. Its venom is so strong it can even kill an elephant. A human who is bitten will die in less than an hour unless medical treatment is given. But the king cobra will attack only if it or its nest is threatened.

King cobras live in the jungles of India, southern China, and the mainland and island countries of southeast Asia. Their diet consists mainly of snakes. They even eat other poisonous snakes!

Like other cobras, when the king cobra is frightened or excited, it will rear up and spread the loose skin on its neck into a "hood." This is the position from which it often attacks. It propels its body forward and sinks its short fangs into its prey.

King cobras are the only snakes that build nests for their eggs. The nests, which are made out of leaves, grass, and other vegetation, are duplex, or two-story, structures. After laying its 18 to 40 eggs on the first floor, the female retires to the second floor. From here she keeps a close watch on the eggs. The newborn snakes are about a foot and a half in length. Their coloring is jet black, with light yellow stripes. As they get older, their color will become a lighter olive brown or gray.

Wood Cockroach
Ectobius sp.

Diet: fresh and decaying plant matter; dead animals
Method of Reproduction: egg layer
Home: Europe and Massachusetts
Length: ½ inch

Order: Mantids
Family: German, brown-banded, and wood cockroaches
Superorder: Cockroaches, termites, and grasshoppers

 Forests and Mountains

 Arthropods

© E.R. DEGGINGER / COLOR-PIC INC.

Although they resemble house roaches in size and shape, wood cockroaches are not indoor pests. They live beneath fallen leaves and ferns in woods and grasslands throughout Europe. One species, *E. pallidus*, traveled aboard Portuguese sailing ships to Massachusetts and still lives there today.

Between June and September, female wood cockroaches produce a brown egg case, called an ootheca, that is about ⅛ of an inch in size. This is huge by cockroach standards. Using her slender legs, the female rotates the egg case and then picks it up. She carries the case for one or two days and then leaves it in a protected spot on the ground. The eggs lie dormant inside their case all winter. The following spring, the egg case breaks open, and out pour tiny, immature cockroaches, called nymphs.

Although similar in size to the common house cockroach, wood cockroaches can be recognized by a distinct triangular patch on the back tip of their wings. They also have small, dark spots and veins on their stiff wing covers. The wings of the male wood cockroach are longer than the female's. He can flutter short distances if he jumps from a rock or stem or if he takes a good running start. The flightless female is shorter and rounder.

Atlantic Cod
Gadus morhua

Length: up to 3 feet
Diet: fish, crustaceans, worms, and mollusks
Number of Eggs: 3 million to 9 million

Weight: 10 pounds
Home: Atlantic Ocean
Order: Codlike fishes
Family: Cods

 Oceans and Shores

 Fish

© LABAT / JACANA / PHOTO RESEARCHERS

Many people are familiar with the Atlantic cod, if only at the dinner table. Hundreds of millions of tons are caught and sold every year. And humans are not the only species that delight in the taste of Atlantic cod. Many larger fish have been gobbling cod for millions of years. How is it that there are any Atlantic cod left alive? Fortunately, this species has adapted to its popularity. Atlantic cod breed like crazy. A single female lays as many as 9 million eggs a year!

Male cod fertilize the eggs outside of the female's body. First the female lays her eggs on the ocean floor. The male makes his deposit nearby, and his microscopic sperm swim to the eggs and fertilize them. In about a month, the eggs will have grown into larva, each just $\frac{1}{50}$th of an inch long. At this size, all they can do is drift along with the ocean currents. At about three months of age, Atlantic cod are a full inch long and can swim to the ocean floor. There they feed on worms and other invertebrates. They will grow to about a foot in their first year. If it escapes being eaten, a cod can live as long as 30 years and grow to 6 feet long and over 200 pounds.

As fast as they are at replacing themselves, Atlantic cod may be in trouble. Some biologists worry that humans are catching too many, and that cod populations are starting to shrink. If so, the experts say, it may be wise to limit the number of cod that can be pulled from the Atlantic each year.

Coelacanth
Latimeria chalumnae

Length: 5 feet
Weight: 120 pounds
Diet: fish
Method of Reproduction:
  live-bearer

Home: deep waters near
  Madagascar
Order: Coelacanths and
  lungfish
Family: Coelacanths

Oceans and
Shores

Fish

© PETER SCOONES / PHOTO RESEARCHERS

The discovery of a live coelacanth in 1938 caused quite a stir—the fish was a member of an order thought to have become extinct 70 million years ago! Fossilized coelacanths are most often found in shallow waters over much of the world, some dating back 70 million to 450 million years. Since 1938 only a few dozen coelacanths have been caught.

This brown-and-blue fish has a number of physical peculiarities that make scientists think it was a distant ancestor to humans, a sort of "missing link." Its pectoral fins seem to be at an evolutionary stage halfway between a normal fin and a walking limb. The coelacanth also has a "swim bladder," thought to be a primitive breathing organ similar to a lung. It has a hollow spine made of cartilage instead of bone, and its heart is simpler than most fishes'. Its stomach is just a large bag, and its intestine is a spiral valve similar to the type found in sharks.

The coelacanth lives in deep undersea cliffs where rock walls drop 10,000 feet to the ocean floor. The enormous (4-inch-diameter) eggs hatch within the mother, who then gives birth to live young. From the day they are born, baby coelacanths creep across deepwater ridges in search of food. Coelacanths are active carnivores. They are equipped with sharp teeth and fight fiercely when hooked.

Rooster-tail Conch
Strombus gallus

Length: 4 to 7 inches
Diet: algae
Number of Eggs: more than 100,000

Home: western Atlantic Ocean from the Carolinas to Brazil
Order: Megogastropod snails
Family: Conch shells

 Oceans and Shores

Other Invertebrates

© DINO SIMEONIDIS / PETER ARNOLD, INC.

The magnificent rooster-tail conch is a valuable collector's item as much for its beauty as for its rarity. Many of the creatures are taken from the western Atlantic Ocean each year, threatening the survival of the species, which has never been abundant.

The rooster-tail's shell has a showy outer lip that extends high above the main body of the shell—much like the tail of a rooster. The edge of the lip is flared and rippled along the side. Most rooster-tail conches are cream-colored with brown streaks, although some rare individuals are purple. The inner surface of the shell is a pearly white, shading to a shiny orange on the inside edge of the outer lip. This large shell is surprisingly lightweight. The male rooster-tail conch is usually larger than the female.

The conch shell is home to a sea snail. The head of the snail peeks out from under the shell on the opposite side from the rooster tail. The creature has a long, fleshy snout that it sweeps back and forth in search of food. At the bottom of the conch's snout is a raspy tongue, used to scrape algae off rocks and other hard surfaces. At the back of the snail's muscular foot is a special clawlike limb called an *operculum*. Conches move by digging this claw into the ground and thrusting themselves forward. They camouflage themselves by cementing broken shells and stones to their own shells.

Devonshire Cup Coral
Caryophylla smithii

Diet : plankton and dissolved organic matter
Method of Reproduction: egg layer

Height: ½ to 1¼ inches
Home: Atlantic Ocean
Order: Stony corals
Family: Solitary corals

Oceans and Shores

Other Invertebrates

© DOUGLAS P. WILSON / FRANK LANE PICTURE AGENCY / CORBIS

Although the Devonshire cup coral is named after a coastal region in Great Britain, it lives on *both* sides of the mid-Atlantic Ocean. This solitary coral builds its own protective case out of calcium in the water. (By contrast, colonial corals protect themselves by fusing together to form a large communal body.) The Devonshire coral anchors the base of its cup-shaped home to a rock or other hard object.

Inside its calcium shell, the soft, fleshy body of the coral polyp (each individual coral animal) is thin, transparent, and colorless. So the polyp itself becomes invisible when it is fully withdrawn into its shell. When the coral wants to come out of its shell, it slowly pumps up its soft body with water. This pumping action unfurls the polyp's 12 shimmering tentacles. Each tentacle stretches up to ⅓ of an inch and ends with a thick, rounded knob.

In bright tropical waters, Devonshire cup corals grow close together in thick patches that become part of coral reefs. In cooler, darker waters, the coral occurs singly or in scattered groups, usually attached to rocky walls, stones, and seashells. Like other coral animals, this species feeds largely by filtering tiny bits of food from the water. The Devonshire cup coral is one of the easiest species to keep in a marine aquarium, because it simply feeds on the leftovers of other aquarium animals.

Large Star Coral
Montastrea cavernosa

Colony Size: up to 36 inches
high, 60 inches wide
Diet: microscopic plants and
animals
Methods of Reproduction:
sexually and asexually

Home: Caribbean Sea and
Gulf of Mexico
Order: Corals and sea
anemones
Family: Stony corals

 Oceans and
Shores

 Other
Invertebrates

The large star coral is a very small creature with a body that resembles a hollow bag. The only opening is at the top. This "mouth" is surrounded by tentacles armed with poison cells. The tentacles capture tiny organisms, called plankton, and bring them to its mouth. The plankton are forced into the hollow central cavity, where they are digested. Parts that cannot be digested are expelled through the mouth.

Star corals form colonies on or near underwater reefs in warm seas. Each coral animal removes limestone (calcium carbonate) from the surrounding sea to build a hard, cuplike skeleton around itself. The cup around each animal in a large star coral is about ⅛ inch deep and ½ inch wide. The cups of neighboring animals fuse together to form a large structure. Young animals build their cups atop those of animals that have died. In this way the colony gets bigger and bigger. It is amazing to think that all the animals in a star coral are related to one another. The colony forms by budding. A small swelling, or bud, forms on the side of one animal. This bud grows into a new animal that makes buds of its own.

Some coral animals grow from eggs. Each eggs becomes a larva, which moves through the water until it finds a hard surface on which to live. If it is successful, it will bud and give rise to a new star-coral colony.

Northern Stony Coral
Astrangia danae

Length of the Colony: 2 inches
Diameter of the Individual: ¼ inch
Diet: plankton, small crustaceans, and fish

Width of the Colony: 4 inches
Number of Eggs: unknown
Home: Cape Cod to Florida
Order: Stony corals
Family: Stony corals

Oceans and Shores

Other Invertebrates

The northern stony coral is quite unusual among its kind in that it thrives outside tropical waters. Though it is found off the coast of Florida, it is most common from Long Island Sound up to Cape Cod. It is also known as the star coral, for each individual coral animal looks like a star. These "stars" live in constellations of as many as 30 individuals. The entire colony is surrounded by a hard calcium skeleton that protects it like a fortress wall. After a colony dies, bits and pieces of its skeleton wash up along the beaches of the East Coast.

This species is one of the many creatures that work the night shift in the world of the coral reef. After sunset the individual northern stony corals stretch out their soft tentacles. They scoop up plankton from the water and blindly grab for tiny young fish larvae and crustaceans. If a creature is too large to fit into its mouth, the stony coral surrounds the prey with special fingers that digest the meal outside its body.

Unlike many corals, the northern stony variety does not sting. Its only defense from predators is to retreat into its hard fortress. Fortunately for the coral, it does not make much of a meal, so it has few enemies. It is, in fact, a great friend of both fish and humans. It helps to build coral reefs, which protect our beaches from erosion and provide a safe, food-rich home for thousands of species of sea creatures.

Red Precious Coral
Corallium rubrum

Height of the Colony: 4 to 20 inches

Width of the Branches: up to 1½ inches at the base

Method of Reproduction: egg layer

Diet: plankton

Home: Mediterranean Sea and the coast of Japan

Order: Sea shrubs, fan corals, red corals, and their relatives

Family: Precious corals

Oceans and Shores

Other Invertebrates

© KURT AMSLER / JACUNA / PHOTO RESEARCHERS

When you put on a piece of coral jewelry, chances are you're wearing red precious coral. People have been collecting and selling this type of coral since the time of the Stone Age. It has been used to decorate shields and swords, to ward off evil spirits, and simply to make its wearer look beautiful. As a result, this Mediterranean coral has become rarer and rarer. To worsen the situation, the slow-growing precious coral is easily injured or killed by pollution.

The coral seen in jewelry and decoration is actually the skeleton of an entire population of tiny creatures called polyps. Coral polyps can't survive independently. They live as a colony, joined together by a hard skeleton. The center of the skeleton is made up of calcium, like human bones. The calcium is surrounded by a tissue called coenenchyme.

Red precious coral is made into jewelry by stripping off the coenenchyme and polishing the calcium "bones" beneath. Its beautiful color comes from iron compounds embedded in the calcium skeleton.

Red precious coral is different from the kind that forms coral reefs. Reef corals have much harder skeletons and so make better building material. Red precious coral is usually found living on hard limestone and volcanic rock—between 150 and 650 feet below the surface of the ocean. In contrast to reef coral, red precious coral survives at depths where little light penetrates.

Staghorn Coral
Acropora cervicornis

Height: up to 10 feet (coral growth)
Width: up to 5 feet (coral growth)
Method of Reproduction: egg layer (coral polyp)

Home: Caribbean Sea, Bahamas, and Florida Keys
Order: Sea anemones and corals
Family: Stony corals

  Oceans and Shores

Other Invertebrates

© STEPHEN FRINK / CORBIS

Rising from a shallow part of the ocean floor are what seem to be growths of bumpy deer antlers branching out in every possible direction. Brightly colored fish swim between the branches. Snails crawl along them. And algae develop at the base of the growths. These growths are staghorn corals. They are the skeletons of coral polyps, tiny animals that live in the sea.

Coral polyps are related to jellyfish. And like the jellyfish, they have very soft bodies. They make these outside skeletons, or shells, for protection. When the polyps die, only the skeletons are left. Many billions of these skeletons form coral reefs and coral islands. Different kinds of coral polyps make different types of coral.

Coral polyps live in colonies. Each coral may reach a height of 10 feet and a width of 5 feet. Its body is shaped like a tube. There is an opening at the top of the tube, and around the opening are tiny tentacles that are equipped with poison stingers, or nettles. These are used to gather food from the sea. At the other end of its body, the polyp has a foot, which is connected to the skeleton.

Coral polyps are egg layers. When the eggs first hatch, the polyps swim around much like young jellyfish. But they soon attach themselves to other coral polyps in the colony.

Star Coral
Astroides calycularis

Length of the Polyp: about ⅕ of an inch
Diet: plankton and small jellyfish
Home: Mediterranean Sea

Method of Reproduction: egg layer
Order: Stony corals
Family: Colonial corals

 Oceans and Shores

Other Invertebrates

© JOSE B. RUIZ / NATURE PICTURE LIBRARY

A colony of star corals looks like a round, thickly branched bush. Tightly packed along the coral branches are what look like feathery flowers. Actually, each "flower" is a coral animal called a polyp. Anchored inside a hard little cup, each soft star coral polyp waves its bright tentacles in the water to catch floating food. The tentacles contain stinging cells that paralyze tiny prey, such as plankton and young jellyfish.

Many hundreds of polyps join together to form a star coral colony. The colony itself may be up to 2 feet wide and 2 feet high. By comparison the familiar staghorn coral of the Caribbean Sea stands up to 10 feet high and 5 feet across. Unlike tropical corals such as the staghorn, the star coral does not form reefs. In the Mediterranean, star coral colonies can be found perched on rocks several yards below the surface of the water.

A star coral colony contains both male and female polyps. In order to reproduce, the males release their sperm into the water. The sperm falls over the female polyps and fertilizes the eggs inside their cups. The offspring look like fuzzy little balls that float through the water until they mature into crawling larvae. The larvae look for hard surfaces upon which they can attach. They mature into adult polyps and then divide to form an entire colony.

New England Cottontail
Sylvilagus transitionalis

Length: 14½ to 19 inches
Weight: up to 3 pounds
Diet: grass, bark, leaves, and other vegetation

Number of Young: 3 to 8
Home: eastern United States
Order: Hare-shaped animals
Family: Hares and rabbits

 Forests and Mountains

Mammals

© MICHAEL P. GADOMSKI / PHOTO RESEARCHERS

The New England cottontail, as well as other cottontail rabbits, was named for the patch of white fur on the underside of its tail. It looks like a ball of white cotton was stuck there. Its body fur, though, is brownish with dark specks.

Like most other rabbits, the New England cottontail is an excellent hopper. It can cover up to 15 feet in one leap. But with a top speed of only 15 to 20 miles per hour, it is not too fast. Swift foxes and other animals, as well as birds of prey, can easily catch this small mammal. And because the New England cottontail is a crop-eating pest, farmers, and gardeners, as well as hunters, kill untold thousands of them every year. Pet rabbits may live for 10 years. But those in the wild are lucky to live for one year. Nevertheless, there are still very large numbers of New England cottontails in New England and south to the Allegheny Mountains. The reason for this is simple. Cottontails have four or five litters of between three to eight offspring every year. Some of these offspring go on to have their own litters when they are only nine or ten months old.

New England cottontails live in woods and areas with lots of brush where they can hide. They eat grass, leaves, and other vegetation. During the winter, they even eat bark and twigs.

Cream-colored Courser
Cursorius cursor

Length: 7¾ to 9½ inches
Diet: insects and other invertebrates
Home: northern and eastern Africa, the Middle East, and southwestern Asia

Weight: 4 to 7 ounces
Number of Eggs: 2 or 3
Order: Waders and gull-like birds
Family: Coursers and pratincoles

 Deserts

 Birds

© ROGER TIDMAN / CORBIS

The pale feathers of the cream-colored courser are perfect camouflage against the desert sand. This handsome bird is much easier to spot in the air. From below, the bold black-and-white markings on the underside of its wings are very apparent. On the ground the courser can be recognized by its distinctive eye stripes.

Although it can fly rapidly, the cream-colored courser prefers to run on the hot desert sand. Between sprints the bird stops to crouch low, hiding from its enemies. Before taking off again, the bird stretches high on its tiptoes, craning its neck to look in every direction. The courser has good reason to be on the lookout for danger. It is a tasty morsel in a barren land where food is scarce. The bird's enemies include vipers, foxes, and desert cats.

The cream-colored courser is itself an efficient little predator. It can gobble down a beetle or grasshopper with a quick jab of its bill—while never slowing from a run. It also busily overturns rocks and digs in the dirt for termites and worms.

At nesting time, the female cream-colored courser simply lays her eggs on the ground. She must stand over them during the heat of day. Her body provides shade from the sweltering sun. When nighttime temperatures fall, she nestles over the eggs to keep them warm.

Bush Cricket (Bush Katydid)
Tettigonia sp.

Length: about 1½ inches
Method of Reproduction: egg layer
Home: North America, Europe, Asia, and northern Africa

Diet: mainly plants
Order: Grasshoppers and their relatives
Family: Long-horned grasshoppers

 Forests and Mountains

 Arthropods

© KIM TAYLOR / BRUCE COLEMAN INC.

Bush katydids, known as bush crickets in Europe, are vividly colored grasshoppers with long antennae. The European bush cricket's sparkling green wings extend far beyond the end of its abdomen. The female appears to have a long stinger at the end of her body. This appendage is really an "ovipositor," or egg-laying organ.

The most familiar European species is the great green bush cricket. In North America, its closest relative is the green chaparral bush cricket of California's Sierra Nevada mountain range. More widespread is its cousin, the fork-tailed bush katydid, which is found near meadows and marshes throughout the United States.

Although they are sometimes seen during the day, bush crickets are essentially nocturnal creatures. The males generally sing their nightly song—"kadydid, kadydidn't"—from the tops of bushes and trees. The females are silent.

Chirping is vital to a bush cricket courtship. The female has a tiny, drumlike ear on each front leg, near her knee. The ear vibrates in response to the male's song. Males have a similar, but simpler, type of ear that enables them to hear their competitors. When bush crickets mate, the male places a ball of sperm at the end of the female's ovipositor. She then deposits her fertilized eggs on various plants.

Set Index